Jenny Ackland

Fun With Colours

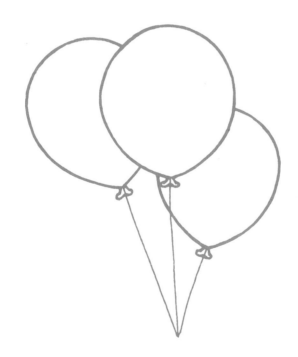

OXFORD
UNIVERSITY PRESS

KU-350-963

Introduction

These workbooks introduce and reinforce basic numeracy and literacy concepts for pre-school and Reception Year children. They give children opportunities to develop some of the skills that act as a springboard for the Foundation Stage Profile, an assessment which teachers complete on each child before he or she moves into Year 1. The activities should be fun and are designed to stimulate discussion as well as practical skills. Some children will be able to complete activities alone, after initial discussion; others may benefit from adult support throughout.

Fun With Colours offers a variety of activities which will help children to recognize five colour names: red, blue, green, yellow and black. The activities are designed to develop the following skills:

- visual discrimination
- hand-eye coordination
- judgement of similarity and difference
- recognition of colour words
- recognition of numbers
- awareness of shape.

Oxford University Press
Great Clarendon Street, Oxford OX2 6DP

Oxford University Press is a department of the University of Oxford.
It furthers the University's objective of excellence in research, scholarship, and education by publishing worldwide in
Oxford New York Auckland Cape Town Dar es Salaam Hong Kong Karachi Kuala Lumpur Madrid Melbourne Mexico City Nairobi New Delhi Shanghai Taipei Toronto

With offices in
Argentina Austria Brazil Chile Czech Republic France Greece Guatemala Hungary Italy Japan Poland Portugal Singapore South Korea Switzerland Thailand Turkey Ukraine Vietnam

Oxford is a registered trade mark of ©Oxford University Press in the UK and in certain other countries

© Oxford University Press 2006
Database right Oxford University Press (maker)
First published 2006

All rights reserved. No part of this publication may be reproduced, stored in a retrieval system, or transmitted, in any form or by any means, without the prior permission in writing of Oxford University Press, or as expressly permitted by law, or under terms agreed with the appropriate reprographics rights organization. Enquiries concerning reproduction outside the scope of the above should be sent to the Rights Department, Oxford University Press, at the address above

You must not circulate this book in any other binding or cover and you must impose this same condition on any acquirer
British Library Cataloguing in Publication Data
Data available

ISBN-10: 0-19-838570-6
ISBN-13: 978-0-19-838570-7

Pack of 6
ISBN-10: 0-19-838571-4
ISBN-13: 978-0-19-838571-4

Pack of 36
ISBN-10: 0-19-838572-2
ISBN-13: 978-0-19-838572-1

1 3 5 7 9 10 8 6 4 2

Designed by Red Face Design
Illustrations by Ivan Ripley and Mark Brierely
Printed in China

PACKS ARE NOT YET PUBLISHED.

Contents

Colour chart

Colour the squares in the right colour.

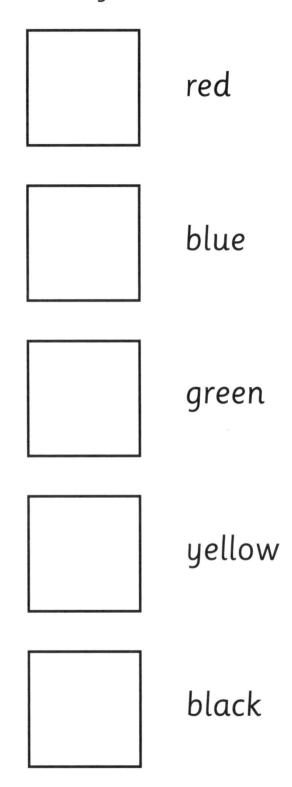

red

blue

green

yellow

black

Note: This chart can be cut out and glued on a piece of card
for the child to use throughout the workbook.

Red

Colour the fruit red.

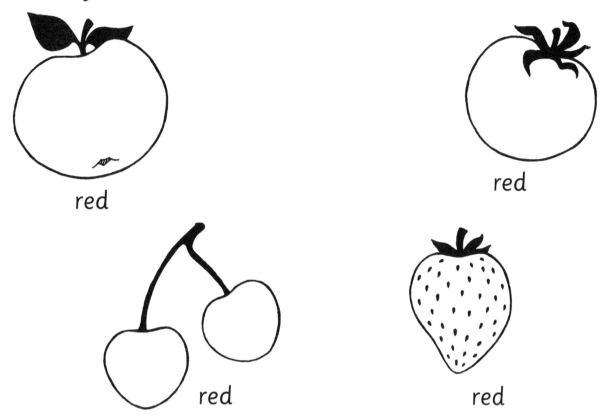

red

red

red

red

Draw red lines.

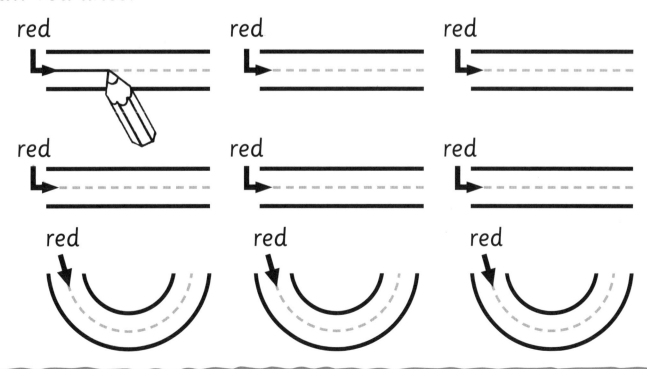

red

red

red

red

red

red

red

red

red

Blue

Colour the balloons blue.

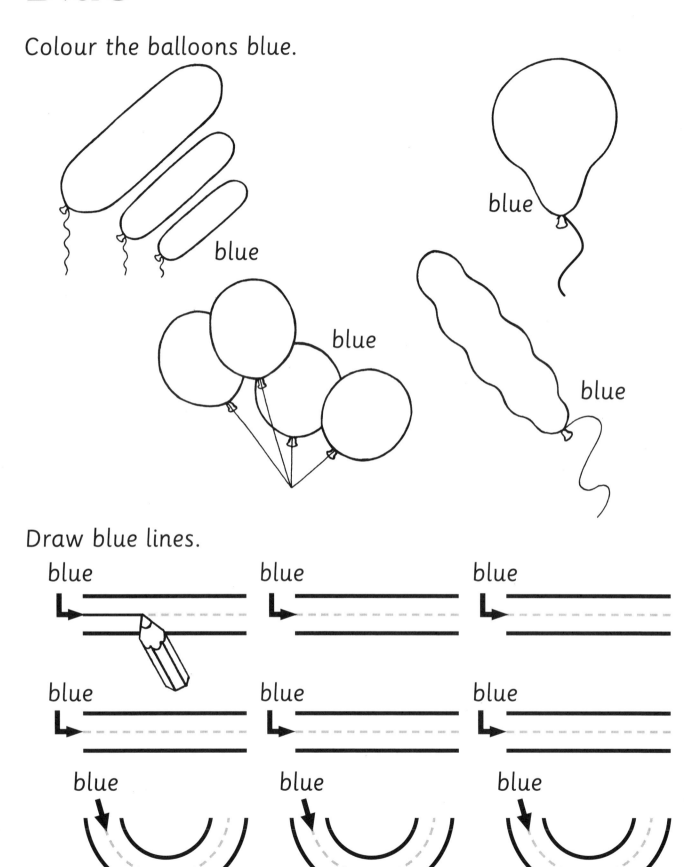

blue

blue

blue

blue

blue

Draw blue lines.

blue

blue

blue

blue

blue

blue

blue

blue

blue

Red and blue

Colour the jugs.

Draw the lines.

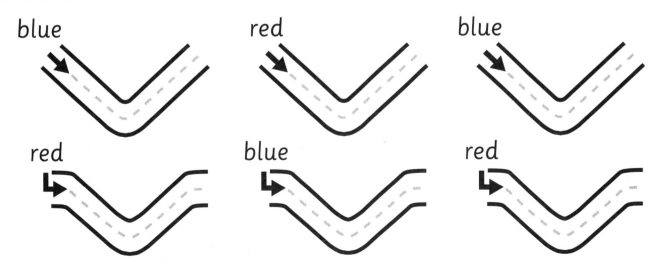

Matching pairs

Colour each pair the same colour.

red

blue

red

blue

red

Matching Pairs

Join up the pairs and colour them the same.

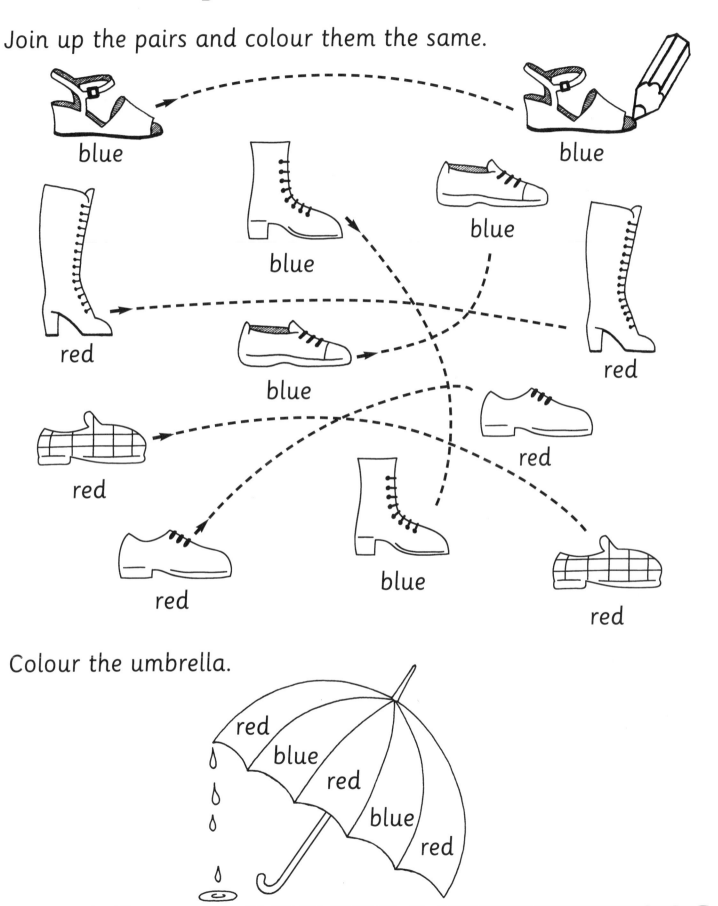

blue

blue

blue

red

blue

red

blue

red

red

red

blue

red

Colour the umbrella.

red

blue

red

blue

red

Green

Colour the shapes green.

Draw green lines.

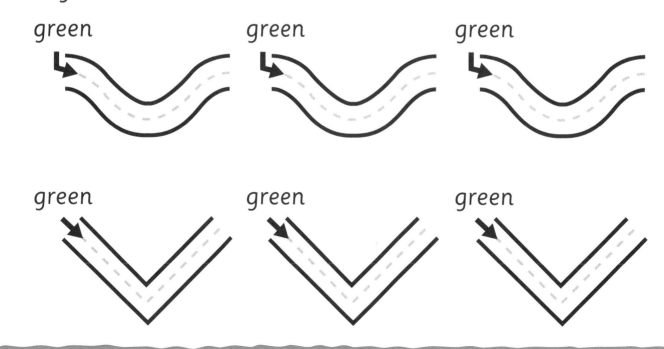

green green green

green green green

Matching pairs

Join up the pairs and colour them the same.

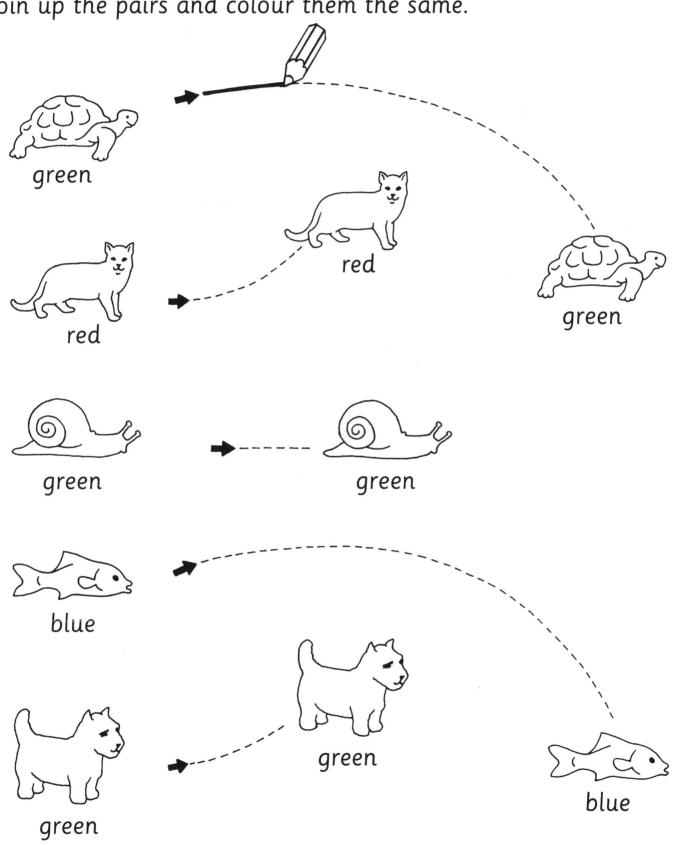

green

red

green

red

green

green

blue

green

blue

green

Red, blue and green

Colour the pictures.

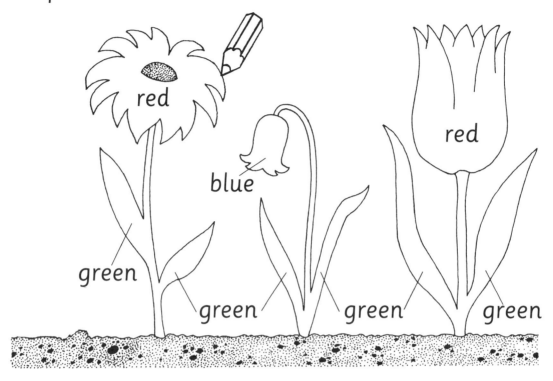

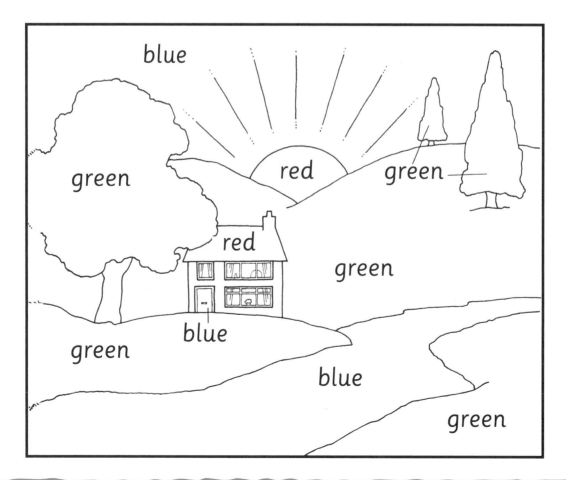

Red, blue and green

Colour the pictures.

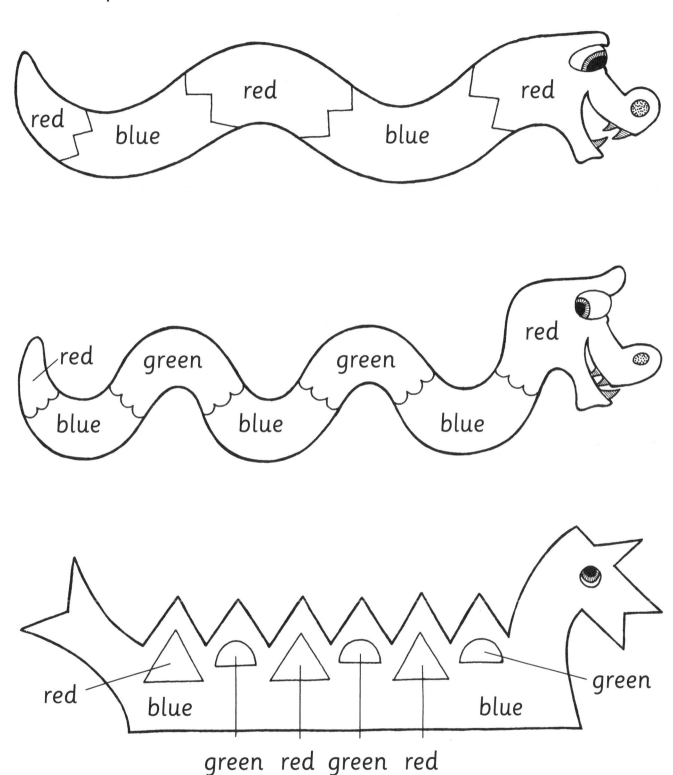

Colours and numbers

Colour the numbers and pictures.

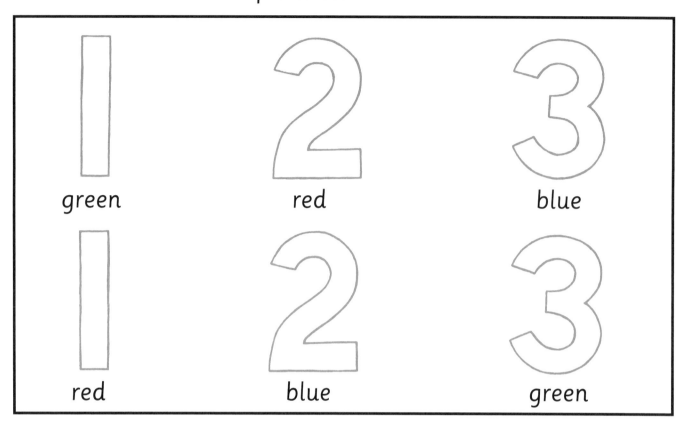

green   red   blue

red   blue   green

green   red   blue

green   blue   red

Red, blue, green and yellow

Colour the pictures.

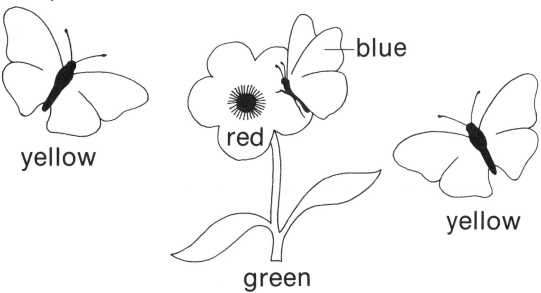

yellow

blue

red

green

yellow

Draw the lines.

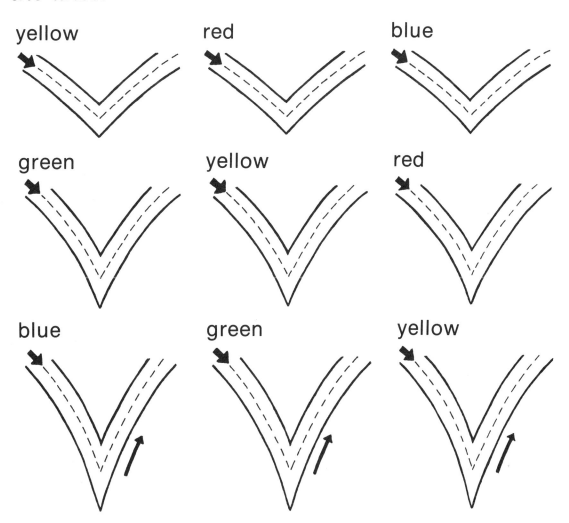

yellow

red

blue

green

yellow

red

blue

green

yellow

Colours and counting

Draw the lines in the numbers.

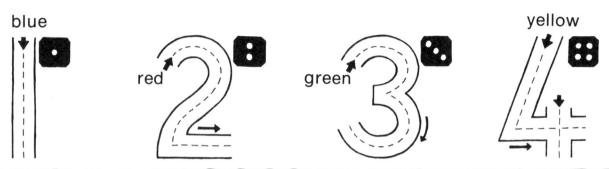

Circle the number of mushrooms in each row.

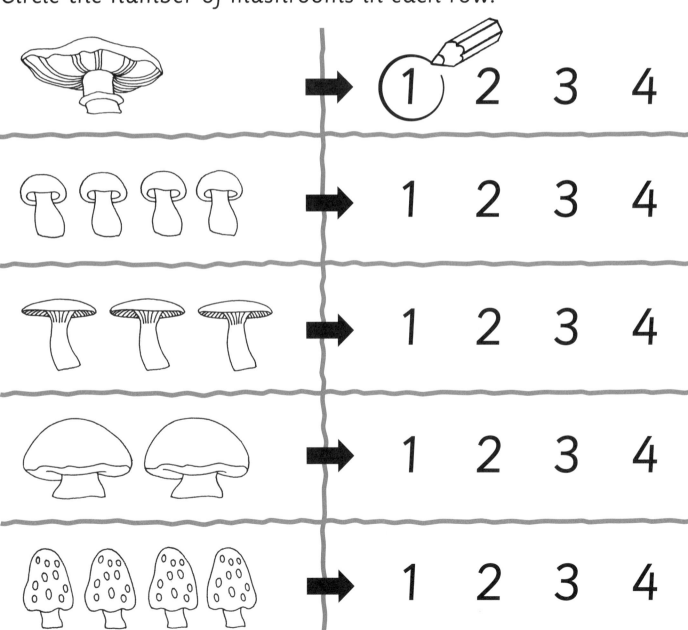

Black, yellow, red and green

Colour the pictures.

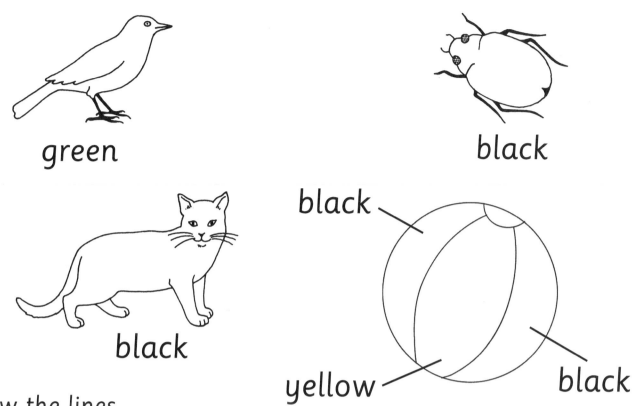

green

black

black

black

yellow

black

Draw the lines.

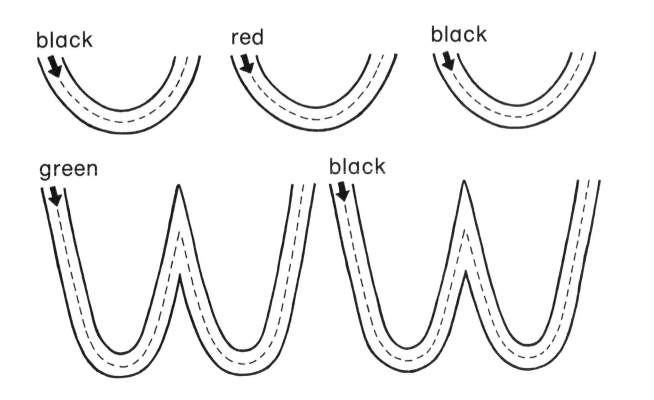

black

red

black

green

black

Colours and numbers

Draw the lines in the numbers.

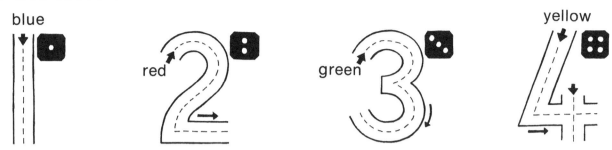

Colour the balloons.

Count them and circle the right number.

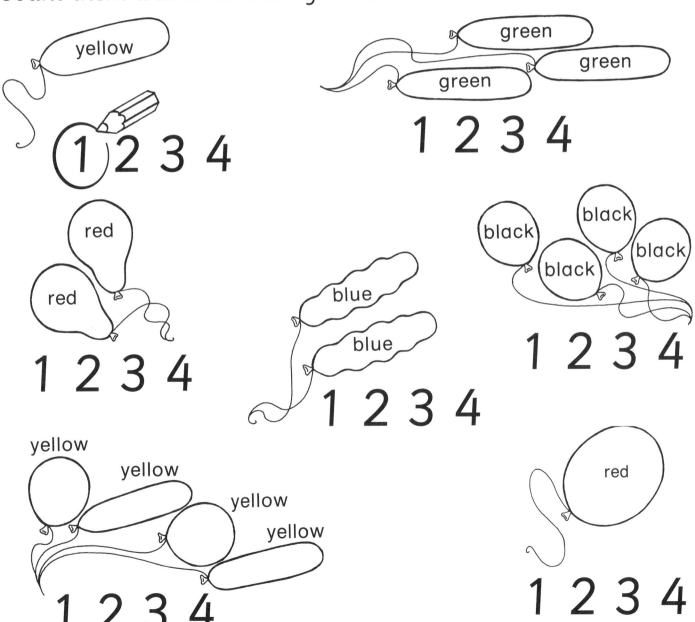

Matching pairs

Join up the pairs.
Colour each pair the same colour.

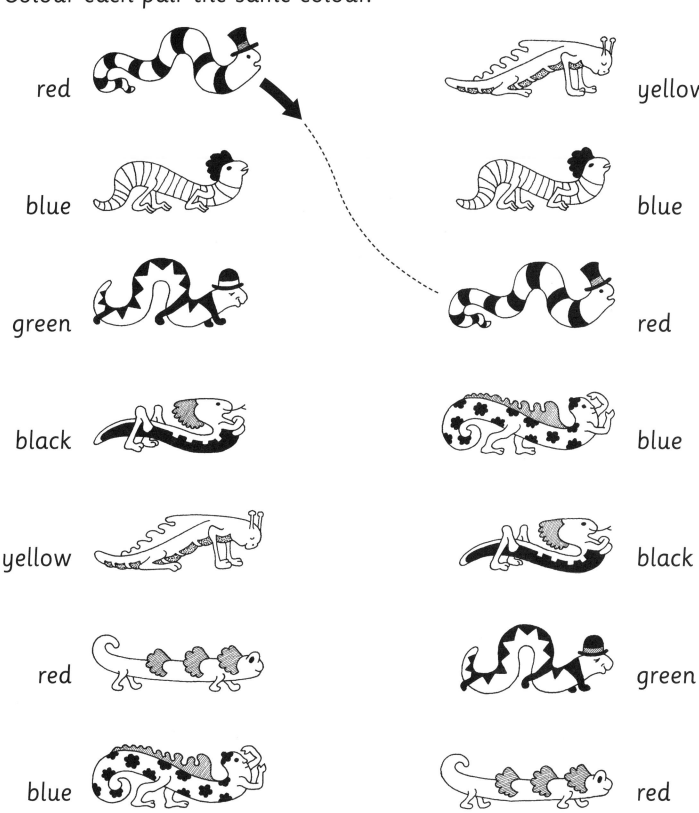

red

blue

green

black

yellow

red

blue

yellow

blue

red

blue

black

green

red

Red, green, blue, yellow and black

Colour the picture.

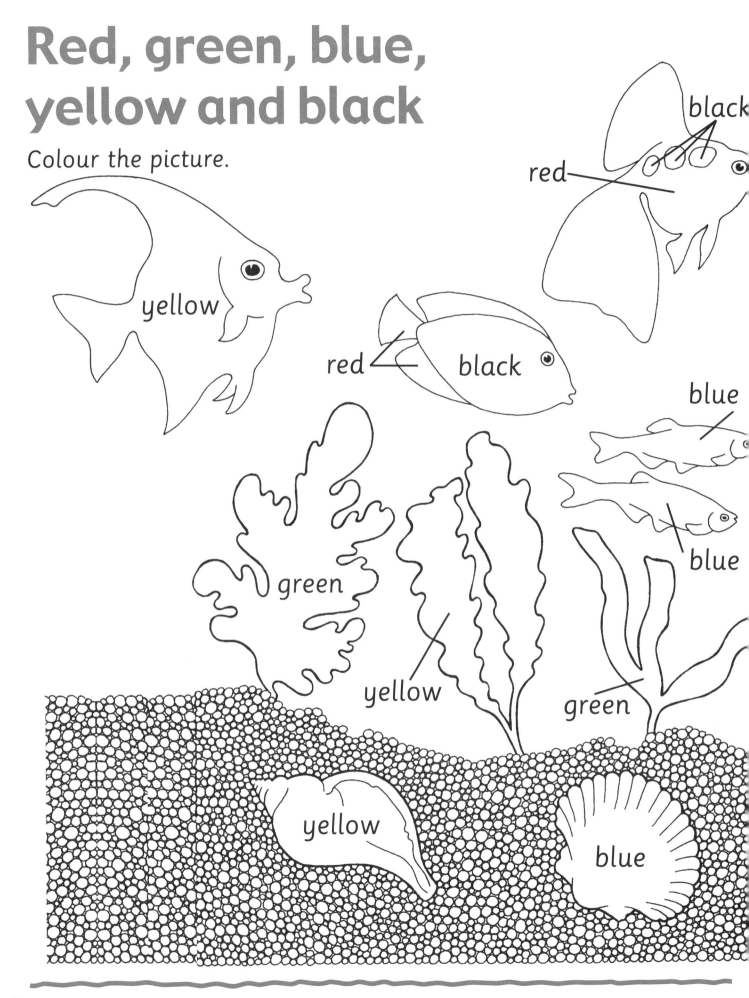

black

red

yellow

red

black

blue

blue

green

yellow

green

yellow

blue

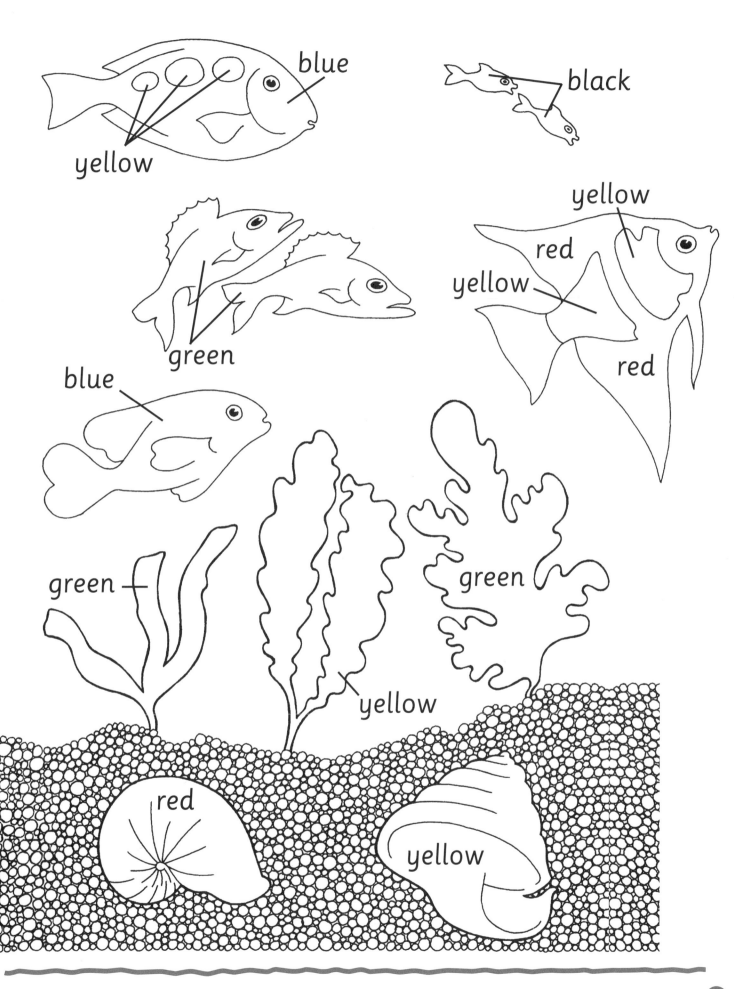

Colour words in sentences

Colour the odd one out red.

Colour the odd one out blue.

Colour the odd one out yellow.

Colour the odd one out green.

Colour the odd one out black.

Colour words in sentences

Colour the fish. Then circle the number of fish in each row.

Colour the three fish blue.

➡ 1   2   ③   4   5

Colour the two fish yellow.

1   2   3   4   5

Colour the four fish black.

1   2   3   4   5

Colour the five fish blue.

1   2   3   4   5

Colour the one fish red.

1   2   3   4   5

Colour the three fish blue.

1   2   3   4   5

Colour the five fish yellow.

1   2   3   4   5

Colour coding

What holds rubbish? Colour it black.

What sucks up dust? Colour it yellow.

What tells the time? Colour it blue.

What holds drinks? Colour them green.

What is used for sweeping? Colour them red.

Colour maze

Colour the pictures.

red · blue · black · yellow

green · red · green

blue · black · yellow · red

blue · yellow · blue

yellow · red · black · green

Help the dog find a path to the bone.
Help the rat find a path to the cheese.

Colours and numbers

Draw coloured spots in the boxes.

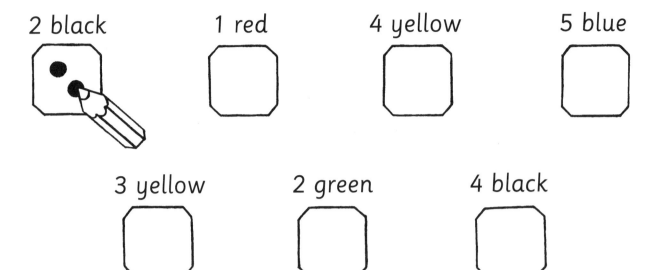

2 black   1 red   4 yellow   5 blue

3 yellow   2 green   4 black

Draw coloured spots on the ladybirds.

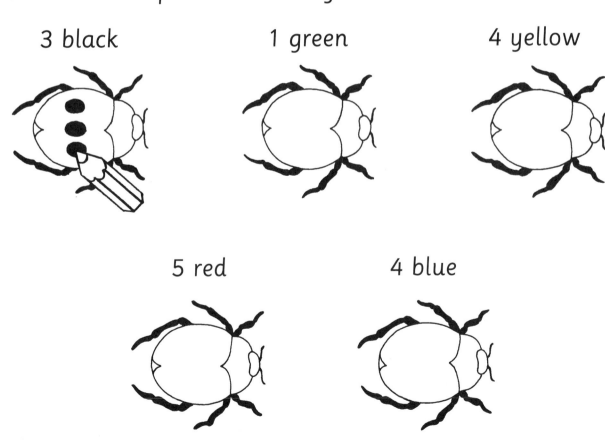

3 black   1 green   4 yellow

5 red   4 blue

Colours and shapes

Join up the matching shapes.
Colour each pair the same.

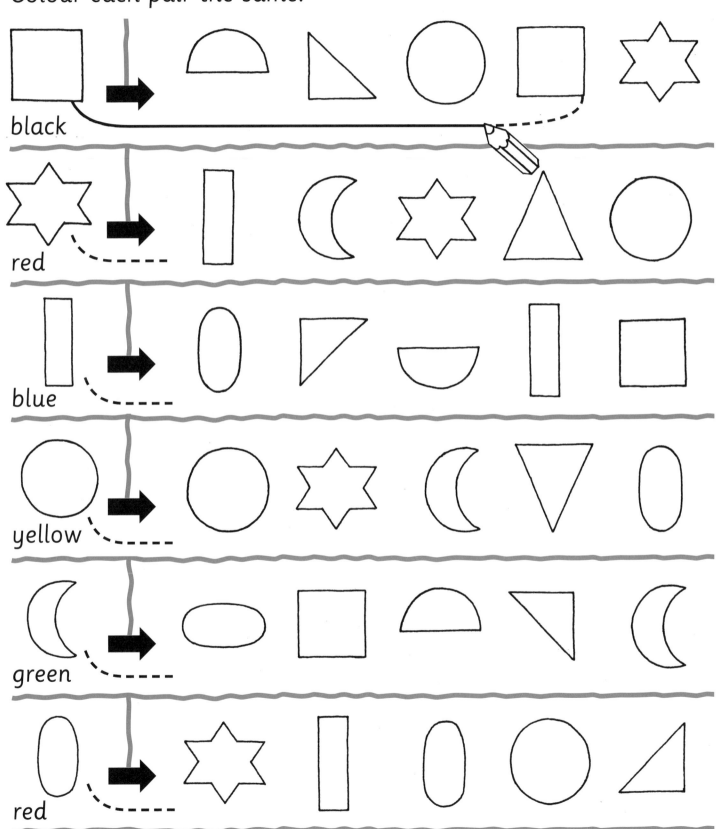

black

red

blue

yellow

green

red

Colours and shapes

Join up the matching shapes.
Colour each pair the same.

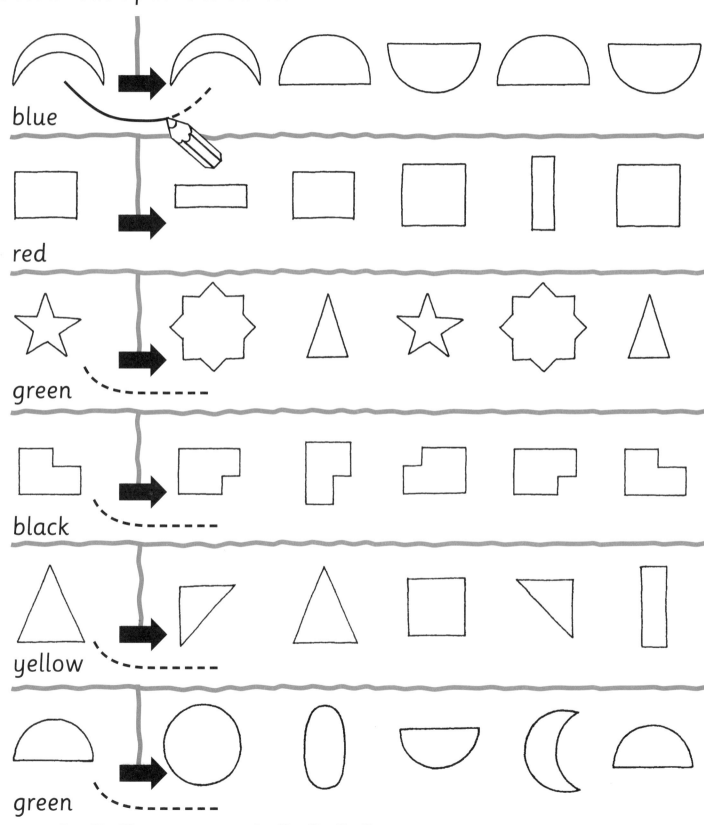

blue

red

green

black

yellow

green

Odd one out

Colour the odd one out black.

Colour the odd one out blue.

Colour the odd one out yellow.

Colour the odd one out green.

Colour the odd one out red.

Colours and numbers

Colour the dots and the numbers.

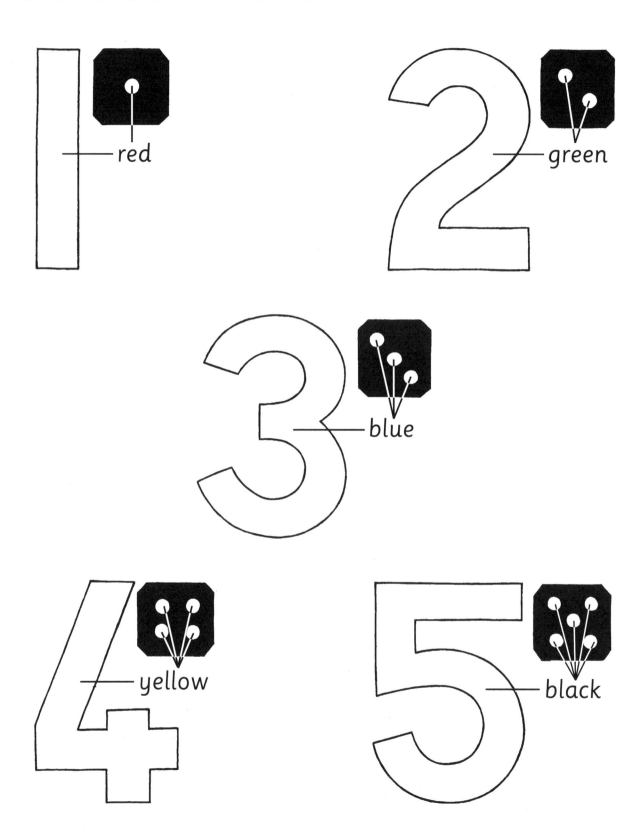

1 — red

2 — green

3 — blue

4 — yellow

5 — black

Colour maze

Colour the fish. Then help them find their way to the bowl that has the same number of fish in it.

black

blue

green

red

yellow

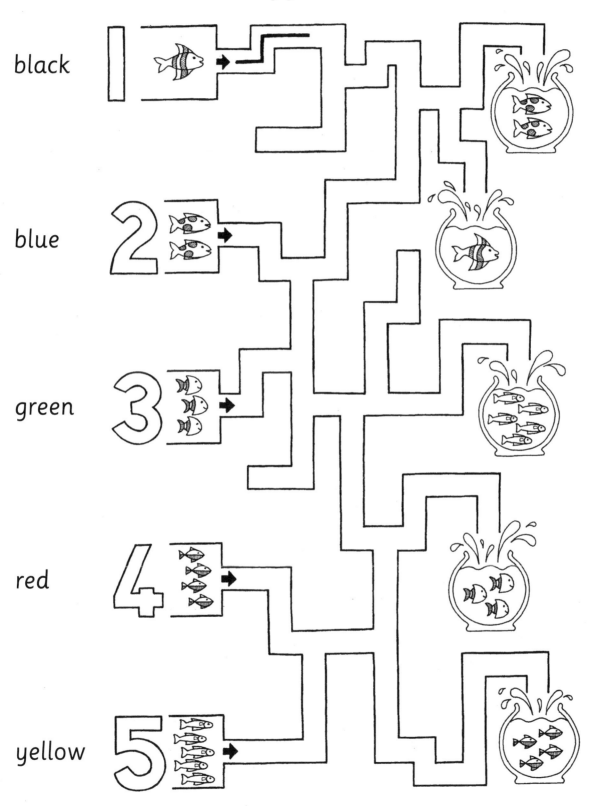

Summary of skills

Fun With Letter Forms
Pack of 6
ISBN-10: 0-19-838581-1
ISBN-13: 978-0-19-838581-3
Pack of 36
ISBN-10: 0-19-838582-X
ISBN-13: 978-0-19-838582-0

Fun With Pattern and Shape
Pack of 6
ISBN-10: 0-19-838575-7
ISBN-13: 978-0-19-838575-2
Pack of 36
ISBN-10: 0-19-838576-5
ISBN-13: 978-0-19-838576-9

Fun With Sounds and Rhymes
Pack of 6
ISBN-10: 0-19-838578-1
ISBN-13: 978-0-19-838578-3
Pack of 36
ISBN-10: 0-19-838579-X
ISBN-13: 978-0-19-838579-0

Fun With abc
Pack of 6
ISBN-10: 0-19-838568-4
ISBN-13: 978-0-19-838568-4
Pack of 36
ISBN-10: 0-19-838569-2
ISBN-13: 978-0-19-838569-1

Fun With Colours
Pack of 6
ISBN-10: 0-19-838571-4
ISBN-13: 978-0-19-838571-4
Pack of 36
ISBN-10: 0-19-838572-2
ISBN-13: 978-0-19-838572-1

PACKS ARE NOT YET PUBLISHED.